#12
John C. Fremont Branch
6121 Melrose Avenue
Los Angeles, CA 90038

W9-BRT-316

THE BIOSPHERE

THE BIOSPHERE
REALM OF LIFE

GREGORY L. VOGT, Ed.D.

TWENTY-FIRST CENTURY BOOKS · MINNEAPOLIS

Twenty-First Century Books
A division of Lerner Publishing Group
241 First Avenue North
Minneapolis, MN U.S.A.

Website address: www.lernerbooks.com

Library of Congress Cataloging-in-Publication Data

Vogt, Gregory.
    The biosphere : realm of life / by Gregory L. Vogt.
        p.   cm. — (Earth's spheres)
    Includes bibliographical references and index.
    ISBN-13: 978-0-7613-2840-7 (lib. bdg. : alk. paper)
    ISBN-10: 0-7613-2840-8 (lib. bdg. : alk. paper)
    1. Life (Biology)–Juvenile literature. 2. Biosphere–Juvenile literature.
    I. Title. II. Series: Vogt, Gregory. Earth's Spheres.
    QH501.V64 2007
    570—dc22   2006018321

Manufactured in the United States of America
1 2 3 4 5 6 – DP – 12 11 10 09 08 07

CONTENTS

LIVING WORLD

Everywhere we look, we see life. From the tops of mountains to the depths of oceans and even within the pores of rocks are millions upon millions of different kinds of life. Earth is a living planet, and its inhabitants owe their existence to the special place Earth occupies in the solar system.

Earth is the third planet from the Sun. It is a modest-sized world only about 8,000 miles (13,000 kilometers) in diameter. It would hardly attract the attention of a passing alien spaceship except for its mild temperatures. Earth is 93 million miles (150 million km) from the Sun, and its surface temperature averages 60°F (16°C). This makes Earth just the right distance from the Sun to have liquid water on its surface. It is neither too hot nor too cold. It is just the right temperature to keep water from completely freezing or completely boiling away. The temperature is also just right for a myriad of chemical reactions that bond atoms into simple and complex molecules—the building blocks of life.

There is much to learn about Earth. It is an incredibly complex system of solids, liquids, gases, and electromagnetic fields. Earth is a world of concentric spheres (like the layers of an onion). The innermost spheres are called the core and mantle. The core is made up of solid and molten metal. The mantle contains rock that slowly flows with great currents of heat. Above the mantle is the lithosphere, or crust, of Earth. The lithosphere is composed of the cool layers of rock and soil we walk on. All the water on Earth makes up the hydrosphere. Water fills the great and small basins of the lithosphere to make oceans and lakes. It flows across the land and occupies the holes in porous rock.

Surrounding Earth is an envelope of gas called the atmosphere. Movements of air and water through the atmosphere are what we call weather. We finally come to the nearly invisible outer atmosphere. Here Earth interacts with the Sun's energy and the environment of space.

Lastly is the living part of Earth. This is the shell of life that extends about 5 miles (8 km) below sea level into the deepest ocean basins and into porous lithosphere rock

THE EARTH'S LAYERS

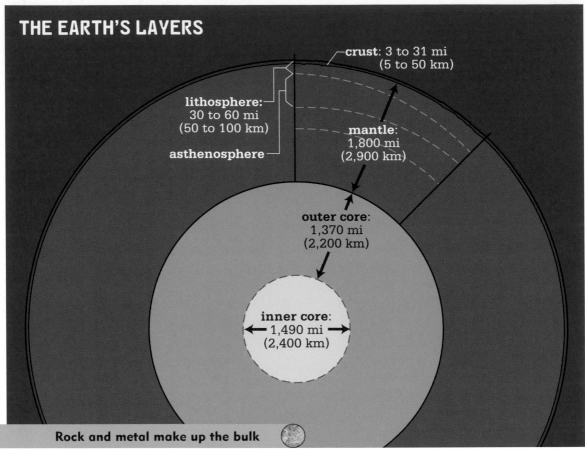

crust: 3 to 31 mi
(5 to 50 km)

lithosphere:
30 to 60 mi
(50 to 100 km)

asthenosphere

mantle:
1,800 mi
(2,900 km)

outer core:
1,370 mi
(2,200 km)

inner core:
1,490 mi
(2,400 km)

Rock and metal make up the bulk of the Earth, but surrounding its massive inner layers are thin layers of water, air, and living things.

and extends upward about 5 miles (8 km) to the mountaintops. It is the most dynamic and fragile of Earth's spheres, and it is called the biosphere. It is the realm of living things and the subject of this book.

CHAPTER 1

WHAT IS LIFE?

Earth is home to an estimated thirty million different kinds of living things. Nobody knows the exact number, in part, because many living things are very tiny and haven't been discovered or studied yet. Life ranges in size from the giant redwood tree more than 360 feet (110 meters) tall to tiny bacteria so small that twenty-five thousand of them lined up would stretch only 1 inch (2.5 centimeters). Life, large or small, literally covers almost every square inch of Earth's surface. Microscopic life—life that can only be seen with a microscope—is found everywhere. Some thrive within rock pores, others within the scalding water of hot springs, and others between the ice crystals in snowfields.

Life takes many forms. Sometimes life is very dramatic, like the surfacing of a great blue whale in the Pacific Ocean. Sometimes life is nothing more than a slick greenish coating on an ocean shoreline rock or a puff of powderlike spores drifting in the wind. At times, life can be very difficult to recognize.

Scientists first need to consider how they define life. What makes a tree different from a rock? What makes a jellyfish different from seawater? These questions are complicated because of the similarities between living and nonliving things. Take a rock and a tree, and grind each down until they each are nothing more than piles of atoms. You will discover the tree and the rock have many of the same kinds of elements. The piles may be so similar that you might not be able to tell which is which. So what makes them different from each other when they are in the form of rocks and trees?

THE DEFINITION OF LIFE

What is life? The answer to this question is both easy and difficult. On the easy side, we can say that life is anything that is living. The hard part is understanding what the word *living* means. The best way to approach it is to describe the characteristics of living things.

If you spread a pocketful of change on a table and sort through the coins, you will get an idea of what scientists have to do to determine the characteristics of living things. You separate the pennies from the nickels and the nickels from the dimes. Then you look for similarities. All the coins are round and flat. All are made of metal. All have raised pictures on their surfaces and so on. If there is a button in the pile, you know that even though it is round and flat, it is not a coin because it doesn't share all the coin's characteristics.

Scientists have examined thousands of kinds of living things and have come up with a list of the characteristics of life. The list is so well thought out, it can be used to separate living from nonliving things. If an unknown thing has all the characteristics of living things, then it is living. Generally, if it is missing one or more characteristic, it is nonliving.

CHARACTERISTICS OF LIVING THINGS

Here are the characteristics of life that scientists have come up with. To be classified as living, an object has to share all five of these characteristics.

1. **Living things are made up of one or more individual units called cells.**

   A cell is a microscopic lump of liquids and solids that is contained inside some sort of barrier, or membrane, that separates it from other cells. The functions of living things, such as growth, reproduction, and using energy from the environment, take place in cells. A living thing can consist of a single cell. Single-celled organisms are called unicellular (uni means "one"). Examples of unicellular life include amoebas and protozoans. The only way you can see most of these organisms is with a microscope.

   Living things with more than one cell are called multicellular (multi means "many"). You are an example of a multicellular organism. You have trillions of cells in your bones, muscles,

Amoebas are examples of unicellular life. They consist of just one single cell.

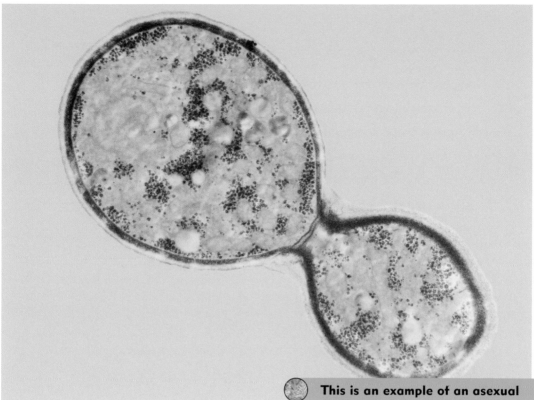

This is an example of an asexual reproduction in a *Cryptococcus* cell. The cell is reproducing itself by dividing itself in two. Soon, the two organisms will divide again and become four and so on.

skin, and blood that work together as a team to make you the way you are. Only living things have cells, but some nonliving things, such as a wooden bookshelf, contain the remains of cells because the wood was once a part of a living plant.

2. Living things reproduce their kind.

Because all living things eventually die, groups of similar organisms, called species, must have a way of producing more of their kind. This is called reproduction. There are two kinds of reproduction. Sexual reproduction requires two cells from different individuals to come together. A cell from your mother and a cell from your father united to form the first cells that eventually grew to become you. Most common living things, such as trees, birds, wheat, dogs, and insects, reproduce this way. The other kind of reproduction is called asexual, and that means that a single organism reproduces itself. Some unicellular organisms, such as amoebas and paramecia, simply divide to produce two copies of themselves.

3. Living things grow and change.

We are all familiar with growth and change. For instance, an acorn is buried and forgotten by a squirrel. Roots sprout and a stem pokes above the soil. Leaves appear and make food from sunlight, water, and gases. After many years, the acorn becomes a towering oak tree that drops new acorns to reproduce itself. The acorn was the seed that developed roots, a trunk, branches, and leaves. You have changed a great deal too. Just look at one of your baby pictures.

Some nonliving things can grow too. The mineral quartz will grow into a six-sided prism shape with pointed pyramids on its ends. A quartz crystal can get quite large and heavy. But there is a difference between this and a living thing. Living things take in water, gas, and nutrients from their environment and grow from the inside out. The quartz crystal grows from the outside as one new layer of quartz atoms is laid on top of another. It doesn't develop new structures as the oak did.

LIVING OR NONLIVING

Sometimes, when we get sick, we say we caught a virus. A virus is an extremely tiny noncellular particle composed of genetic material and proteins. When a virus infects a cell, it can cause serious diseases such as smallpox or meningitis. Although biology books often classify viruses as living things, many scientists who study viruses do not consider them living. According to cell theory, living things are composed of cells. By that definition, viruses are nonliving. Yet, viruses are composed of proteins and genetic material. What do you think?

4. Living things obtain and use energy from the Sun or from other living things.

All living things need to carry on life processes. In your case—and that of all animals—obtaining energy is a matter of eating. The food you eat contains energy. The energy comes from the Sun. Plants collect the Sun's energy and convert it, along with water, gas, and minerals from the soil, into leaves, stems, seeds, and fruit. When we eat plants, we convert the plant materials back into energy to power our bodies and use the nutrients contained in the plants for growth. Most living things on Earth get their energy either directly

MAKING FOOD

Gardeners have been perplexed by one big question. When they plant a kernel of corn, a tall cornstalk with several ears and thousands of new kernels is produced. The initial seed was tiny. Where did the entire plant come from? In the seventeenth century, Dutch physician Jan van Helmont devised an experiment to find out. He measured the mass of a small seedling and the mass of the pot of soil he planted it in. For five years, he watered the seedling. By the end of his experiment, the seedling had become a tree weighing 165 pounds (75 kilograms). The mass of the pot of soil was almost the same as when the experiment started. Van Helmont concluded that the mass of the tree came from the water he had added to it.

Van Helmont was only partially correct. A later experiment by British chemist Joseph Priestley showed that plants give off oxygen. A Dutch scientist, Jan Ingenhousz, showed that Priestley's discovery only worked when plants were exposed to sunlight. These experiments and others convinced scientists that plants were doing something remarkable. They were using the Sun's energy, carbon dioxide gas, and other nutrients from Earth to grow and to make the food that animals depend upon.

Jan van Helmont, a Dutch physician, studied plants. He wanted to find out how a tiny seed of corn could turn into a tall cornstalk with new kernels. He concluded that water is what makes plants grow. Later experiments showed it was not only water but the Sun and carbon dioxide gas that help plants grow.

This photo shows a "black smoker" vent in the ocean floor. Vents like this allow some organisms to grow without light.

from the Sun or from the things they eat. However, some unusual organisms live around hot water spewing from deep ocean water vents. These organisms grow without light, using the sulfur compounds in the mineral-rich water.

5. Living things respond to changes in their environment.

Responding to changes in the environment is a survival skill that all living things possess. It is one of the most obvious characteristics of life. A car approaches, and you step out of the way. On a hot day, you perspire and the sweat evaporating from your skin helps keep your body from overheating. On a cold day, shivering helps keep you warm.

Plants move their leaves to track the Sun as it crosses from east to west. Plant roots grow downward in response to gravity and stems grow upward. A hawk soars the sky while watching for a rabbit or mouse to break cover. Deer will seek the woods for cover during the heat of the day and walk out into clearings to graze in the cool dimness of the evening. A chameleon will change its color to blend in with its background as a protection from predators. Living things sense odors, light, colors, sounds, gravity, temperature, water, and pressure to improve their chance for survival. They do so to maintain healthy conditions in their bodies so that they can continue to live. This process is called homeostasis.

To summarize, living things are made of cells, reproduce their own kind, grow and change from the inside, obtain and use energy, and sense and respond to their environment. It is these five characteristics that separate a tree from a rock. The tree does all these things. The rock does none of them.

CHAPTER 2

KINGDOMS OF LIFE

A biologist studies life on Earth. One of the challenges these scientists face is to distinguish one kind of life from another. It is a big challenge because of the millions of different kinds of living things on Earth.

Biologists have determined that all known life falls into six major categories called kingdoms. Knowing which category a particular living thing falls into can tell you much about what that living thing is like and how it lives. The kingdoms most generally accepted by biologists are the Eubacteria, Archaea, Protista, Fungi, Plantae, and Animalia. You can probably guess which kingdom you belong to—along with dogs, cats, birds, snakes, and elephants. Some of the other kingdoms have names that may be a bit mystifying.

THE SMALLEST LIFE: KINGDOMS OF EUBACTERIA AND ARCHAEA

The smallest living things are microscopic, meaning that they can only be seen as individuals under a microscope. Organisms in the kingdoms Eubacteria and Archaea are microscopic.

Eubacteria and Archaea are tiny unicellular organisms. The eubacteria are the organisms we are always trying to destroy with antibacterial soap and antiseptic for first aid. Members of these two kingdoms are the life-forms that cover nearly every square inch of the surface of Earth. The Eubacteria group is the larger of the two kingdoms. Eubacteria are very tiny, from about 0.00004 to 0.0004 inch (0.001 to 0.01 millimeter) long. Some eubacteria live in the soil, and some infect larger organisms, causing disease. They're shaped like tiny pill capsules, and many have small fibers sticking out of their sides. The fibers wiggle, enabling the creatures to move and roll.

Some eubacteria use the Sun's energy to make their own food. They live in both freshwater and salt water. Some varieties survive in extremely hot water, such as the water of a hot spring, while others live on the surface of snow. After a great natural disaster, such as a volcanic eruption that kills off local life with hot lava flows, eubacteria are often the first organisms to return to the area when things cool off.

Archaea are the "tough guys" of the microscopic world. They thrive in the harshest environments, such as the digestive tracts of animals, thick mud, very salty water such as the Great Salt Lake in Utah, and around hot springs where the temperatures can peak at 190°F (88°C). Some members of this group live under the

CAVE SLIME

You have probably heard of stalactites and stalagmites, but have you heard of snottites? Snottites are oozy, drippy, icicle-like drools of slime hanging from the ceilings of some caves. Snottites are made by bacterial colonies that live in caves where hydrogen sulfide gas (rotten egg gas) combines with oxygen to make sulfuric acid. The bacteria produce their own acids that eat into the cave rock. To protect themselves from a really nasty environment, the bacteria secrete a slimy film that covers them up to produce a secure home. When the film and bacteria become too heavy, they start to droop, hence the name snottites. National Aeronautics and Space Administration (NASA) scientists are especially interested in snottites and other cave bacteria. Life, if it exists on other worlds such as Mars, might thrive beneath the surface of the planet. Learning about snottites and other subsurface life will give the scientists ideas about what to look for on other worlds.

GOOD BACTERIA

In spite of our fear of bacteria, many kinds of bacteria are quite useful to us. Certain kinds of bacteria are essential in the creation of many delicious foods and beverages such as cheese, yogurt, sour cream, pickles, and wine. Some bacteria eat oil, making them useful to clean up small oil spills. Others help in the breakdown of dead plant and animal matter, releasing nutrients back into the environment for future living things to use. *E. coli* bacteria live in our intestines. There, they find a warm and safe environment. In return, they help us digest our food and process molecules that we cannot digest on our own. We both benefit from this partnership (with the possible exception of the production of embarrassing methane gas).

E. coli bacteria *(left)* live in our intestines and help to digest the food we eat. *E. coli* also help with molecules we cannot digest ourselves. Not all *E. coli* is good. In 2006, *E. coli* from cattle waste contaminated spinach and led to 199 people becoming very sick and to three deaths.

oceans, around hydrothermal vents. At these deepwater vents, extremely hot, mineral-rich water streams upward from the ocean floor. The water is black with minerals so the vents are known as smokers. Archaea living around these vents live off the sulfur in the water.

KINGDOM PROTISTA

The kingdom Protista is a good deal smaller than the two bacteria kingdoms. Nevertheless, it still includes more than 115,000 members. Protista are unicellular, mostly microscopic organisms, though some are just large enough to be seen with the naked eye. If you have ever looked at a drop of pond water under a microscope, the little swimming things you saw were protists. Protists are more complex than bacteria. Their cells contain a variety of structures including a nucleus and organelles. These structures will be explained in the next chapter when cells are described in more detail.

The kingdom Protista is subdivided into protists that are animallike and those that are plantlike. They are actually neither, but they share similarities with the kingdoms Animalia and Plantae.

Animallike protists are unattached organisms that move freely through water. Some move under the power of hundreds of tiny fibers, or cilia, projecting outward from their cell membranes. The cilia work like the oars of ancient Roman ships to propel the protists around. The cilia also push water containing food particles into a pore, or tiny opening. The food is digested, and waste products are expelled through another pore. Other animallike protists, such as some bacteria, have long, whiplike fibers called flagella that they use to push themselves around.

One group of animallike protists lives within worms, fish, birds, and humans. The protist *Plasmodium* lives

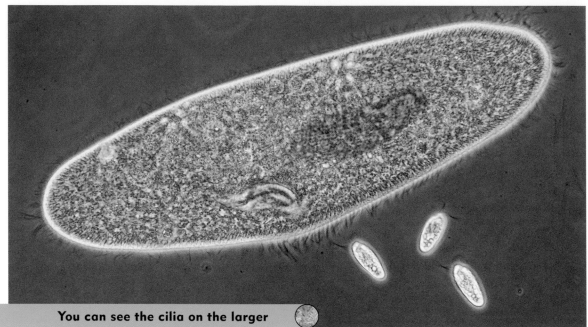

You can see the cilia on the larger of these protists, which wave in the water to move the organism around. The smaller protists have flagella that they use to move around.

inside *Anopheles* mosquitoes. When an infected mosquito bites a human, some *Plasmodium* enter the human's bloodstream and reproduce millions of offspring. In the process, toxins (poisonous chemicals) are produced that lead to chills and fever. This result is a disease called malaria.

Plantlike protists create food from raw materials and the energy in sunlight using a chemical process called photosynthesis. This process depends upon a material called chlorophyll. Chlorophyll is a pigment. It gives plant leaves their green color. The purpose of chlorophyll is to capture the Sun's energy. Think about the last time you went out on a blistering hot, sunny day wearing a black shirt. The black pigments of the shirt absorbed all the rainbow colors in sunlight and made you very hot. If you changed to a white shirt, you would feel cooler because white reflects all the rainbow colors. The green color of chlorophyll is good at absorbing red, blue, and violet light from the Sun.

Once the Sun's energy is absorbed, a complex chemical reaction takes place within the plant cells. This reaction is called photosynthesis. It takes molecules of carbon dioxide and water and turns them into oxygen and a form of sugar called glucose. The photosynthetic process removes carbon dioxide from the atmosphere, makes food, and releases oxygen into the atmosphere. The majority of all living things on Earth depend upon photosynthesis directly or indirectly (by eating other organisms) for life.

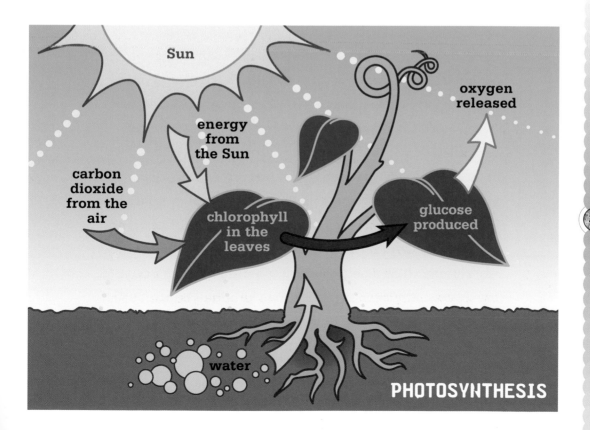

Sun

oxygen released

energy from the Sun

carbon dioxide from the air

chlorophyll in the leaves

glucose produced

water

PHOTOSYNTHESIS

Giant kelp in the waters of the
Pacific Ocean are an example
of phytoplankton.

More than 70 percent of all the
photosynthetic reactions taking place
on the surface of Earth occur within a group of creatures
called phytoplankton. The word *phytoplankton* is used to
describe any photosynthetic organism that lives near the
surface of the ocean. That includes plantlike protists and
giant, algae like sargassum kelp that can grow more than
200 feet (60 m) long. (Although some references consider
only microscopic organisms as phytoplankton, others consider floating plants of any size to be phytoplankton.) One
subgroup of plantlike protists floats in tropical oceans and,
when disturbed, gives off a ghostly blue light. These are
called pyrrophyta or fire protists.

The plantlike protists are vitally important to the
biosphere. Phytoplankton protists produce enormous
quantities of food and oxygen that can be used by other
organisms. Sea creatures from shrimp to giant whales

depend upon protists directly or indirectly for food. When you eat a fish sandwich, you are eating a fish that ate smaller fish that fed on phytoplankton protists.

Phytoplankton protists that are not eaten reproduce and eventually die. Their tiny bodies, which contain minerals absorbed from the ocean during their growth, settle to the ocean floor. The minerals pile up and eventually turn into sedimentary rock that may later be exposed on Earth's surface.

KINGDOM FUNGI

Order a pizza with mushrooms, and you are enjoying fungi. Fungi are organisms that could easily be mistaken for weird-looking plants. They grow from tiny spores and may form a mass of fibers that look similar to roots. They may grow stems, sprout leaflike caps, and produce new spores. Fungi take on many forms, but they are not capable of making their own food. Fungi get their food from decaying dead plant and animal matter or from living organisms.

Fungi are very common, and you can usually find some in your house. When you open an old loaf of bread and find grayish green powdery spots, you are looking at a kind of fungus. Mold on a damp wall is also a form of fungi.

Fungi require a food source. They are essential to re-cycling the nutrients contained in dead matter so other living things can use them again. Fungi help keep Earth's surface from piling up dead matter.

Not all fungi are helpful. Some fungi are parasitic, meaning they get food from a living host and cause damage to it in the process. You might have come across shelf fungi growing from the trunk of a living tree. The tree was

HUMONGOUS FUNGUS

What may be the world's largest organism lives in a forest in eastern Oregon. We are not talking about a tall tree. This organism lives mostly beneath the soil and occasionally sends up mushrooms to the surface. The organism is a monster-sized *Armillaria ostoyae*, or honey mushroom. It is a member of the kingdom Fungi. Grown from a single microscopic spore, the fungus has spread beneath the forest floor for about twenty-four hundred years. It covers an area of around 2,200 acres (890 hectares). The honey mushroom lives off water and nutrients from tree roots, eventually killing them. This sounds bad, but over the long term, the mushroom actually helps the forest by creating new clearings for wildlife grazing. Woodpeckers live in the dead trees. New plants and trees grow as decaying matter is recycled.

A honey mushroom, growing in eastern Oregon, may be the world's largest organism.

When disturbed, these puffballs can release trillions of spores into the air, some of which will reproduce.

probably sick, and the fungi found an easy host to infect.

When fungi reproduce, they manufacture tiny spores that act like seeds. The spores are so tiny that millions of them may look like thin wisps of smoke as they are carried by wind. The giant puffball, a white globular fungus the size of a basketball or larger, can contain seven trillion spores that are ejected into the air when it is disturbed. Most of the spores do not reproduce, so releasing huge quantities of them ensures that a few, at least, will reproduce.

Fungi can even be helpful in the kitchen. Bread is made with fungi called yeast. Yeast is a single-cell fungi that when watered and fed sugar and flour produces tiny carbon dioxide bubbles. These create the little holes in the bread that give it its texture and shape.

KINGDOM PLANTAE

All members of the kingdom Plantae are multicellular organisms. They have cells that contain the chemical cellulose. Cellulose is a very tough, fibrous material found in the cell walls of plant cells. It gives support to plant stems, enabling them to stand up from the soil.

Cellulose is also the principal component in the paper of this book.

Plants, such as flowers, vegetables, grasses, mosses, and cacti, all share the ability to use photosynthesis to make their own food from water, carbon dioxide, and sunlight. Plants take many forms but generally have a few things in common. They have some sort of root system to anchor themselves to a particular place, stems to raise themselves upward to compete for sunlight, and structures such as leaves or needles that have chlorophyll to capture sunlight. Land-based plants get their water from the soil and carbon dioxide from the atmosphere. Water-based plants, such as ocean kelp, absorb the carbon dioxide that is dissolved in seawater.

The country of Brazil is believed to be home to more than fifty thousand species of plants. The United States is home to only eighteen thousand species.

KINGDOM ANIMALIA

Creatures in the kingdom Animalia are what we usually associate with life. Dogs, birds, worms, fish, frogs, bears, insects, spiders, tigers, whales, humans, and many more are animals. The diversity of the kingdom Animalia is incredible. Think of giraffes, bats, platypuses, porcupines, butterflies, jellyfish, armadillos, skunks, manta rays, and anacondas. All have unique ways of living.

Animals eat plants or animals that eat plants to obtain energy. They have some sort of digestive system that breaks down their food into nutrients and releases energy for growth and to power movement. Part of the digestive process involves oxygen, which helps to break down food. Animals breathe in the oxygen released by plants. In turn, animals exhale carbon dioxide that plants use in photosynthesis.

Animals are multicellular. Unlike plant cells, animal cells do not have tough cell walls made of cellulose. Instead, they have soft membranes that separate one cell from another. More than any other life-forms, members of the kingdom Animalia have complex subsystems to perform specialized jobs. For example, insects and spiders have hard shells to provide shape and protect their bodies. Other animals have internal skeletons that provide support for the soft parts of their

The world's largest spider is the goliath spider, which is nearly 12 inches (30 cm) across.

If you ever come across a dangerous snake on a cold day, don't worry. The snake absorbs body heat from its surroundings. At temperatures colder than 50°F (10°C), the snake's muscles are so sluggish that it is hard for the snake to move.

bodies that surround them. Some animals have tails that can grasp. Some have wings. Some propel themselves through water with fins. Some have bodies that look like plants to hide themselves from predators.

Animals have sensory systems to monitor changes in their environment. You, for example, can sense light, odors, sound, chemicals (through taste), motion, pressure, temperature, and even the direction of gravity. Not all animals have all the same senses, but the purpose of these systems is to find food, avoid danger, and seek mates for reproduction. Animals also have muscles for movement, a circulatory system to distribute blood and oxygen, a respiratory system to exchange gases with the atmosphere, and a digestive system to process nutrients and remove wastes.

The most amazing members of the kingdom Animalia are the ones reading this book. We are the only members that wonder about how life came to exist and the only ones that have the mental and physical powers to answer that question.

CHAPTER 3

WHERE DID LIFE COME FROM?

One of the oldest of all questions is how did life come to Earth? Of course, to answer how, you also need to answer the question of when. Over the centuries, many answers to these questions have been offered. Some were based on people's beliefs, and some were based on observations of the world.

Scientists are interested in the details—the how. What was the mechanism that produced life? What did the first life look like? In what kind of world did it appear? How did it live and change? Each question breeds hundreds of additional questions. Scientists believe they understand the basic framework leading to the

33

formation of life, but much is left to be learned. Where do we start answering the lifequestion? We start at the beginning, when Earth came into being.

Earth is thought to be approximately 4.6 billion years old. It formed along with the Sun and the planets from a great gaseous cloud of atoms left over from ancient stellar explosions. Gravity pulled most of the atoms in the cloud to the center. As the cloud condensed, it began to swirl. The atoms that fell to the center became the Sun, which ignited in nuclear reactions to produce heat and light. The remaining atoms of the cloud came together to form whirlpools of matter that clumped together to become planets, moons, asteroids, and comets orbiting the Sun.

The early Earth was a blistering hot world of

This artwork shows Earth forming in the early solar system. The inner planets formed by gathering up surrounding material, such as the rocks shown, through gravitational attraction.

molten rock that was continually pelted with space debris. Large and small space rocks and icy comets fell to its surface in a torrent. The heat from the impacts and the heat generated by radioactive elements within Earth kept the planet surface molten for tens of millions of years.

In time, loose debris in the spaces between the early planets began diminishing and the surface of Earth started cooling. Rafts of hardened rock appeared and melted over and over again. Gradually, the rock rafts remained longer and longer. Eventually they merged to form an outer crust surrounding the molten interior.

The ancient atmosphere of Earth was unlike today's atmosphere, which consists primarily of nitrogen, oxygen, and trace gases such as carbon dioxide and water vapor. The atmosphere originally consisted of water vapor, carbon dioxide, carbon monoxide, hydrogen, nitrogen, and probably methane and ammonia. It didn't have free oxygen, which is required to sustain most living things.

Rain fell on Earth, but the surface was still too hot for water in liquid form, so it boiled away as soon as it touched the surface. By 3.8 billion years ago, the surface had cooled enough that pools of water began to collect. As the ground cooled, so did the atmosphere above it. The water vapor it contained condensed into torrential rains that drenched the surface for many years. Comets and icy rocks continued to fall to Earth from space, and the water contained in them added to the oceans that were forming.

Although no one knows when life appeared on Earth, scientists have discovered microfossils, similar to today's bacteria, in rocks that are 3.5 billion years old.

Eventually life appeared, but nobody knows exactly when. Fossils are the remains of ancient life turned to stone. They have been found in rocks that are 3.5 billion years old. The fossils are microscopic and appear to be early forms of bacteria. But the rocks with the earliest fossils may not actually be the starting point for life on Earth. Earth's surface continually changes. Rocks are broken down by weathering and erosion, and new rocks are formed in ocean basins as the debris piles up. New surface material is produced by volcanic eruptions. Rocks with earlier fossils simply may not have survived.

LIFE ON EARTH— THE REAL STORY

The theory of how life formed on Earth can be pretty complicated, and scientists are still struggling with the details. Early Earth had an atmosphere with a complex mixture of elements, including hydrogen, nitrogen, carbon, but no oxygen. The oxygen was locked in molecules so that it was not available for breathing. Exactly what happened to the atmosphere is still a mystery.

SKYSCRAPERS OF ANCIENT EARTH

Shark Bay, Australia, is one of the few places where living stromatolites can be found. Stromatolites are curious clumps of layered rock about 1 to 2 feet (0.3 to 0.6 m) high that include thin surface coatings of cyanobacteria. Fossil stromatolites have been found in many areas of Earth. Geologists have dated some of these fossils back to the beginning of life on Earth—about 3.5 billion years ago.

Stromatolites grow mushroomlike stumps of rock in shallow water. Dust collects on the surface of the bacteria, and the bacteria surround the dust to get to the surface so that they can collect the Sun's energy for growth. More dust collects, and the bacteria migrate around it. Gradually, the dust layers turn to stone. Only the top, hair-thin layer of a stromatolite is alive. The bacteria grow at a rate of about 0.02 inch (0.5 mm) per year. Compared to the size of the bacteria that make them, stromatolites are huge. They are equivalent to humans building a 60-mile-high (100 km) skyscraper!

These stromatolites, looking sometimes like large stony mushrooms, can be found at Shark Bay in western Australia. Fossils of stromalites are among Earth's oldest remains of living things.

Experiments that were done in 1953 gave scientists important clues in explaining the presence of organic molecules on Earth. This is important because all life on Earth is constructed from organic molecules. Since those molecules weren't here when Earth formed, explaining their appearance on Earth is essential to understanding how life developed.

U.S. scientists Stanley Miller and Harold Urey constructed a chamber in their laboratory. They filled the

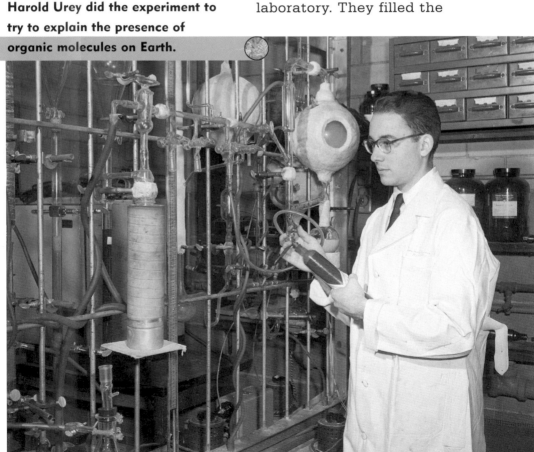

Scientist Stanley Miller in the lab where he created conditions believed to have existed on Earth 3.5 billion years ago. Miller and scientist Harold Urey did the experiment to try to explain the presence of organic molecules on Earth.

chamber with a mixture of gases simulating Earth's early atmosphere. Next, they produced electric sparks in the chamber to simulate the energy from lightning. After a few days, a collector attached to the chamber gathered molecules of several amino acids that had not been there before. Amino acids are important building block molecules for the creation of proteins. Proteins are used in your body to build and repair cells. It is important to note that the experiment didn't create life. It did, however, show that some of the essential compounds for life could have formed naturally from the elements and compounds in the early atmosphere by interacting with lightning.

Following along the lines of the Miller-Urey experiment, scientists think organic compounds formed in Earth's early atmosphere and collected in the oceans to make what scientists call an organic soup. Scientists have discovered that individual amino acid molecules in such a soup tend to naturally link. They gradually grow to form tiny droplets. Some divide and form new droplets. The droplets are not alive, but their division provides hints as to how living cells might grow and divide.

As exciting as the Miller-Urey experiment was, many scientists were not satisfied. Other hypotheses have been advanced to explain the presence of organic molecules on Earth. The molecules could have come to Earth from space. Astronomers have identified those same chemicals in giant gas clouds in deep space. Furthermore, some meteorites that have fallen to Earth contain organic materials. So do comets. In one estimate, modern Earth is pelted with about 40,000 tons (36,000 metric tons) of comet dust every year. The dust is full of organic materials. It covers Earth and gets into everything, including your food. Those molecules are the raw materials of life, but not life itself. They need to be combined in just the right way to become alive.

Regardless of how organic molecules appeared on Earth, what happened next is even more complicated. Somehow, different amino acids joined to become complex proteins. They did so in a way that permitted them to grow, divide, and repeat the pattern again and again. The problem that biologists face in trying to understand what happened is similar to the chicken and the egg puzzle. Which came first? To have an egg, you need a chicken. To have a chicken, you need an egg.

This model of DNA found within living cells shows the complex structure of the molecule.

Similar questions arise when determining what materials formed first in order to produce life. In living things, many materials must be present at the same time to make proteins. Organic molecules called deoxyribonucleic acid (DNA) and ribonucleic acid (RNA), enzymes, and amino acids are needed. DNA and RNA can be thought of as chemical information storage systems for living things. Enzymes are chemicals that speed up reactions in cells. Cells may have hundreds or thousands of different enzymes. Each one speeds up a particular reaction. You need DNA to make proteins, but DNA needs RNA, enzymes, and amino acids to do so. DNA provides the recipe used by the cell to synthesize RNA and enzymes, but DNA needs these things to do so in the first place. Like the chicken and egg puzzle, which came first? Confusing? You bet! Something got it all started, and biologists are still trying to figure it out.

Somehow and at some point, the first true living cells appeared. They resembled some types of bacteria that live today. These early cells required food and probably got it from the organic soup from which they were generated. They lived without oxygen. They were the starting point for all life on Earth. How did they evolve and differentiate to become humans, giraffes, ocean kelp, condors, and butterflies hundreds of millions of years later? At some point, the organic chemicals in Earth's early oceans formed membranes; started adapting to the environment; developed a variety of structures; and learned how to get

DEEPWATER SMOKERS

In 1977 scientists aboard the deepwater submarine *Alvin* dove thousands of feet beneath the Pacific Ocean near the Galápagos Islands. They came upon an opening in the ocean floor from which scalding, chemical-rich water was emerging. The water was black from the chemicals, and the outflow looked like smoke from a dirty smokestack. These thermal vents had been studied before—their environment is so harsh that scientists thought no life could possibly survive there. Yet, this team was startled to find thickets of giant tube worms near the vents. Some of the worms were more than 4 feet (1.2 m) long. The lower end of each worm was planted firmly in the ocean floor, while a red, flowerlike plume at the other end swayed in the current.

In addition to the tube worms were mussels, shrimp, clams, crabs, tiny lobsters, and microscopic archaea. The vents are too deep for sunlight to penetrate, so the living things depend upon archaea to make food from the hydrogen sulfide in the hot water.

One of the ideas of how early life formed centers on these vents. The hypothesis suggests that living things first evolved around ocean floor vents billions of years ago. Earth was volcanically more active back then, and these smokers would have been common. It has been observed that the archaea that thrive around smokers are very much like the early fossils found in 3.5 billion-year-old rocks.

The archaea and the worms living near the smokers have a symbiotic relationship, meaning that both creatures benefit. The archaea live inside the worms and process chemicals from the vent into food for the worms. The food goes directly into the worms through their red plumes because they do not have mouths.

food, reproduce, and function as living beings. How this happened is for future scientists to figure out.

One thing that is certain is that when life did appear on Earth, it began to cause major changes in Earth's environment. The organic chemicals in the oceans began to run out, and an ancient form of photosynthesis evolved. It was very different from today's photosynthesis. Instead of water, chemicals such as hydrogen sulfide were used. Sunlight powered the reaction, and food was produced.

About 2.2 billion years ago, the photosynthesis process changed. Cyanobacteria (also known as blue-green bacteria) started using water in the process and produced oxygen as a waste product. Oxygen is deadly to some forms of life. It can destroy organic compounds. Bacteria that thrive in oxygen-free environments had to retreat from the oceans and Earth's surface. They moved into the deepest places of Earth, where oxygen couldn't reach.

The oxygen released in the new process first saturated ocean water. It reacted with dissolved iron, and for a time, Earth became a rusty planet. The layers of iron ore around the world today are the result of this change in the oceans. The excess oxygen began changing the atmosphere too. Over hundreds of millions of years, the atmosphere, which had had almost no oxygen, became one-fifth oxygen. This set the stage on Earth for the miraculous growth of new life-forms that would follow.

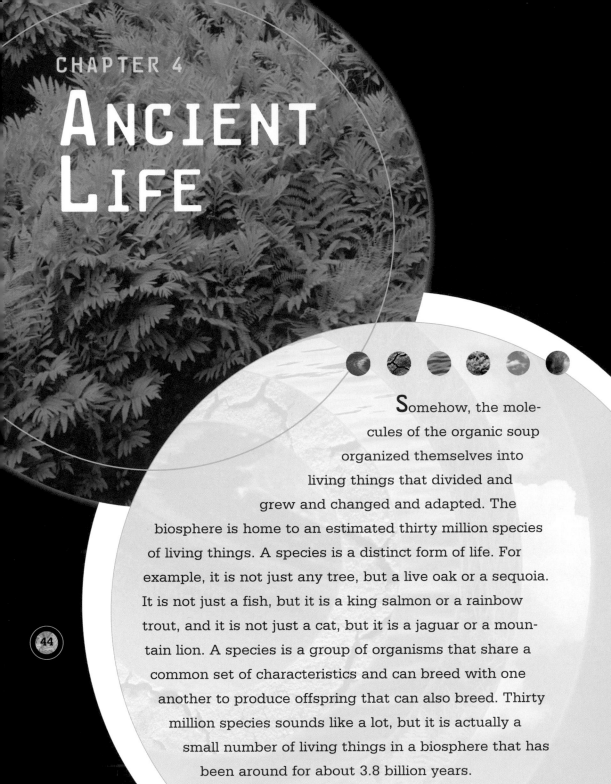

CHAPTER 4

ANCIENT LIFE

Somehow, the molecules of the organic soup organized themselves into living things that divided and grew and changed and adapted. The biosphere is home to an estimated thirty million species of living things. A species is a distinct form of life. For example, it is not just any tree, but a live oak or a sequoia. It is not just a fish, but it is a king salmon or a rainbow trout, and it is not just a cat, but it is a jaguar or a mountain lion. A species is a group of organisms that share a common set of characteristics and can breed with one another to produce offspring that can also breed. Thirty million species sounds like a lot, but it is actually a small number of living things in a biosphere that has been around for about 3.8 billion years.

Scientists learn about ancient life by studying fossils. Fossils are ancient bones and shells or stony impressions. They are found all over Earth, mostly in sedimentary rocks. Sedimentary rocks are a part of Earth's lithosphere. They form when the forces of nature wear away ancient rocks, and the tiny grains that are left over accumulate in layers. In time, the layers are cemented together to form new rock. Dead animals, plants, and even tiny bacteria settle with those grains and are covered up. Gradually, their bodies are replaced piece by piece with minerals and turn to stone.

Paleontologists are scientists who study fossils. Paleontologists have been collecting and classifying fossils for hundreds of years. Like biologists, who can only estimate the

Paleontologists find the remains of a 10-million-year-old rhinoceros at a dig site in Nebraska. Scientists study fossils like this to learn about ancient life on Earth.

number of living species, paleontologists can only estimate the number of species of ancient life. The number is astounding. Earth's biosphere may have hosted several hundred million species of life. More than 99 percent of those species are now extinct (all members of a species are dead).

The record of fossils shows a story of many species of life arising on Earth and then perishing. Scientists have divided Earth's history into a giant calendar of eras, periods, and epochs. The calendar spans the entire history of Earth, about 4.5 billion years. Each segment of the calendar is known for the kind of life that existed then.

The longest pieces of the calendar are the eras. These are like months in the calendar we live by. Earth's calendar has four eras, but they are not of equal length. The oldest era is the Precambrian era, and it begins with Earth's formation from the gas cloud that became the Sun and planets. The first 700 million or so years were too hot for life to exist, but about 3.8 billion years ago, the first single-celled organisms probably appeared. These were the archaea that got their energy from the noxious chemicals that were found in the early atmosphere and oceans. The Precambrian era ended about 500 million years ago. In its last years, multicellular animals such as worms and jellyfish and simple plants appeared. Life learned how to use the Sun's energy through photosynthesis. Earth's atmosphere gradually accumulated oxygen as a waste product of photosynthesis.

Next came the Paleozoic era. This period began an explosion of new species. All kinds of shellfish, corals,

This museum restoration shows
living organisms that lived in
the oceans in the Paleozoic era.

protozoans, trilobites, starfish, sea
urchins, and many more appeared
and inhabited the oceans. Fifty million years into this era,
the first land plants, scorpions, and bony fish appeared.
These were followed by insects, reptiles, spiders, amphibians, and trees.

About 250 million years ago, the Mesozoic era began.
This was the era of the dinosaurs—triceratops,
stegosaurus, tyrannosaurus, parasaurolophus, and others.
These animals were big. They ruled Earth's land for almost
200 million years. But they were not alone. The Mesozoic
also hosted flying reptiles, marine reptiles, alligators, birds,
and the tiny mammals we are descended from.

Last came the Cenozoic era, about 65 million years
ago. During this era, mammals (our ancestors) became
the dominant life on Earth. About 30 or 40 million years
ago, the first monkeys appeared. Early humans appeared
about 5 million years ago. Modern humans are newcom-
ers, appearing only about 130,000 to 200,000 years ago.

BIOSPHERE CALENDAR

(Not all periods are divided into epochs, so the epoch column is sometimes blank.) Chart adapted from "Origins," *NOVA*, PBS, 2004.

ERA	PERIOD	EPOCH	AGE
Precambrian			4.5 billion – 550 million years ago
Paleozoic	Cambrian		550–505 mya
	Ordovician		505–438 mya
	Silurian		438–408 mya
	Devonian		408–360 mya
	Carboniferous	Mississippian	360–325 mya
		Pennsylvanian	325–286 mya
	Permian		286–248 mya
Mesozoic	Triassic		248–213 mya
	Jurassic		213–145 mya
	Cretaceous		145–65 mya
Cenozoic	Tertiary	Paleocene	65–55.5 mya
		Eocene	55.5–33.7 mya
		Oligocene	33.7–23.8 mya
		Miocene	23.8–5.3 mya
		Pliocene	5.3–1.8 mya
	Quaternary	Pleistocene	1.8 mya– 8,000 years ago (ya)
		Holocene	8,000 ya–present

LIFE-FORMS

First single-cell organisms and simple plants. Algae,
bacteria, jellyfish, worms, and sponges

Multicellular organisms abound. Trilobites, clams,
snails, corals, and protozoans

Starfish, sea urchins

First land plants, ferns, sharks, and scorpions

Fish abound. First insects, first amphibians, and first
forests

First winged insects, coral reefs, great forests, and
first reptiles

First cone-bearing trees

Amphibians and reptiles flourish. Trilobites and many
other marine animals become extinct.

First dinosaurs, mammals, turtles, and lizards

First squids, frogs, and birds

First flowering plants and modern fish. Mass extinction kills
dinosaurs and many land and marine animals.

Mammals start to dominate.

Horses, whales, and monkeys

First apes, camels, and elephants

Grazing animals, modern trees, and plants

Early humans and modern sea life

Ice Age, Neanderthals, mammoths, and mastodons

First modern humans

If we could reduce the entire history of life on Earth to a twenty-four-hour clock, modern humans would be represented by only the last second before the stroke of midnight.

To help paleontologists keep track of fossil life, the eras have been further divided into periods. You are probably familiar with the Triassic, Jurassic, and Cretaceous periods. These are the subdivisions of the Mesozoic, or dinosaur, era. Modern humans live in the Cenozoic era in the period called the Quaternary. Some of the periods are further divided into epochs. Our epoch is the Holocene.

WHERE DID THEY ALL GO?

Extinction is an event or series of events, either fast or slow, that leads to the deaths of all members of a particular species. Extinction can be caused by a variety of small and large factors. A species of life with a small population could be driven to extinction simply by a lengthy drought that withers food supplies. Another species might be killed off by an ice age, during which advancing glaciers cover the land and scrape away the habitat that a species depends upon. A new species might appear and feed on an older species and drive it to extinction. Two or more species might compete for the same food supply, causing the less able species to perish. Humans clear large tracts of land, drain swamps, build dams, and release chemicals into the environment. Species that do not adapt will perish. A large asteroid or comet striking Earth would cause massive changes in the environment. Many species would die in its aftermath.

Extinction is going on all the time. As species disappear, others take their place. A few times, however, extinctions have been extensive. At the end of the Cretaceous period, all the dinosaurs became extinct. About 75 percent of other life on the land and in the oceans perished with them. The rapid disappearance of so many species is called a mass extinction.

Scientists debate how many mass extinctions have occurred. There may have been five, six, ten, or even twenty or more mass extinctions. One hypothesis states that Earth experiences a mass extinction

This computer illustration shows dinosaurs watching fragments of a large asteroid colliding with Earth. Scientists think an event like this caused the mass extinction of dinosaurs at the end of the Cretaceous period.

Although dinosaurs have been extinct for 65 million years, many scientists believe their descendants are still around in the form of birds.

when the environment undergoes major changes every 26 million years. The regularity of the extinctions is blamed on a star named Nemesis. You can't find Nemesis on star charts. It is supposed to be some invisible or faint star that swings close to the Sun (or the Sun swings close to it) every 26 million years. Gravity disruption, radiation, or both cause the extinctions. Nemesis is an interesting idea, but its proponents can't locate the star or offer any proof other than that some small mass extinctions seem to have occurred every 26 million years or so. Less fanciful explanations for mass extinctions are more likely.

About 250 million years ago, huge volcanic eruptions in what is now Siberia belched out dust and acid droplets and blocked the Sun's light. The eruptions continued for about 800,000 years, cooling the world. Ice accumulated in polar and mountainous regions, and sea level dropped significantly. Worldwide habitats changed dramatically, and mass extinctions followed.

It is important to remember that extinction is primarily a natural process. It has been going on since the beginning of the biosphere. Today, however, many species are becoming extinct not because of nature but

TAIL OF THE DEVIL

Chicxulub is a small Mexican village on the Yucatán Peninsula of Mexico. Chicxulub is on the opposite side of the Gulf of Mexico from Texas. Most people would not have heard of Chicxulub except for a discovery made in 1991. The remains of a giant crater were discovered nearby. Partly on land and partly underwater, the crater was badly eroded and hard to see. Nevertheless, geologists pieced together a variety of observations and determined the crater was about 110 miles (180 km) wide. It would have taken a 6-mile-wide (10 km) asteroid striking Earth to do the job. Dating techniques put the collision at 65 million years ago, which is at the very end of the Cretaceous period.

The impact must have been catastrophic for all of Earth. It would have triggered massive earthquakes; heated up the atmosphere; and injected millions of tons of ash, dust, water, and sulfur dioxide into the atmosphere. Huge wildfires would have been ignited. Rain would have become strongly acidic. Gradually, the haze in the atmosphere would have cooled Earth by 20 to 30°F (-7 to -1°C).

By the time Earth returned to normal, all the dinosaurs and about 75 percent of all Earth's land and ocean species had become extinct. In spite of the evidence showing the impact occurred at the same time as the extinctions, not all scientists are convinced the impact is the whole story. Massive volcanic activity near India occurred about the same time, and it too would have had an impact on Earth's life.

This artwork shows the impact of an asteroid hitting Earth at Chicxulub, Mexico, 65 million years ago.

because of human activity. Whenever humans compete for the same habitats as other life, humans invariably win out because of technology. Chain saws and bulldozers can level entire forests in a matter of weeks. Oil tanker spills in the ocean wreak havoc on marine birds and mammals. Humans release chemicals into the atmosphere. They are thinning the layer of ozone in the upper atmosphere. Ozone is a form of oxygen that blocks deadly ultraviolet radiation from reaching Earth's surface.

In past centuries, hunting for pelts nearly wiped out the sea otter and seal populations of Alaskan waters. Whales were relentlessly pursued for the oil that could be extracted from their flesh. Exotic feathers worn on women's hats led to the extinction of bird species. Although modern scientists are more aware of how human activities are harming other living things, the destruction of habitat continues.

Rain forests used to cover 14 percent of Earth's land surface. Cutting for farmland has reduced that cover to just 6 percent. At the current rate of cutting, the last rain forests will be gone in 2050.

Human population growth and the quest for food and riches are altering habitats around the world. For example, the rain forest in the Amazon basin in Brazil is home to about 30 percent of Earth's plant and

An aerial view shows the primary rain forest in the Amazon basin in Brazil, home to about 30 percent of Earth's plant and animal species.

animal species. The rain forest is being cut down to make room for roads, dams, pipelines, and small farms. In 2004 alone, construction of a single highway in the rain forest has resulted in the clearing of trees in an area equal to the size of New Jersey.

One important lesson that can be learned from nature is that humans are just as dependent on Earth's environment as any other species on the planet. Humans have been around for only a tiny piece of the history of the biosphere. If human society changes the environment too much, we can drive ourselves into extinction. Humans will then be just a tiny blip in the life calendar of Earth. It would be interesting to see what the dominant life-forms of the next era will be.

CHAPTER 5

GETTING ALONG TOGETHER

From outer space, it is easy to see that planet Earth is a single living system we call the biosphere. Astronauts see dense forests, grasslands, deserts, oceans, lakes, and icy polar regions. Each environment blends into the others. Views of Earth from space have helped scientists understand that human society is part of this living system and absolutely dependent upon it. There is no other place to go. So we have to protect our home. Doing so requires an understanding of how Earth's biosphere works.

When scientists study the biosphere, they first define what life is and examine the different kingdoms of life. They look at the basic units of life, how these units function, and how life has changed over

Earth's history. Yet, to fully understand the biosphere, we must also understand how living things interact with one another and with the nonliving parts of Earth.

Because the biosphere is so complex, biologists prefer to work with smaller units called ecosystems. An ecosystem consists of all the living and nonliving components in a given area, such as a desert or a swamp. The members comprising the living part of an ecosystem are called the community. The community includes everything from microorganisms to fungi, plants, and animals.

When biologists study an ecosystem, they don't just make up a list of the members of the community. They focus on how those members interact with one another. Each community member plays one of three roles: producer, consumer, or decomposer. You can probably guess that the producers are plants and certain microorganisms that use photosynthesis to produce food from sunlight, water, and carbon dioxide.

The consumers are the living things that eat the plants and the microorganisms. Consumers also include the living things that eat the living things that eat the producers. There can be several steps of consumers. For example, if you have a hamburger, you are eating a cow, which ate a producer (grass or grain). However, there are even more steps if you eat a fish. It will have eaten a smaller fish that ate a still smaller fish that ate plankton.

Decomposers are bacteria and fungi that get their energy from dead matter, such as leaves and twigs and dead animals. In the process, the chemicals that made up the plants and animals are changed into forms that can be used by new living things to grow.

FLOWS AND CYCLES

Producers, consumers, and decomposers work together in many ways. Energy, nutrients, gases, and water move in and out of the community in flows and cycles. A flow is a one-way path, while a cycle is a closed path that continues around and around.

Energy from the Sun flows through the ecosystem. Producers make food through photosynthesis. Most of the food (energy) goes to the growth of the producers

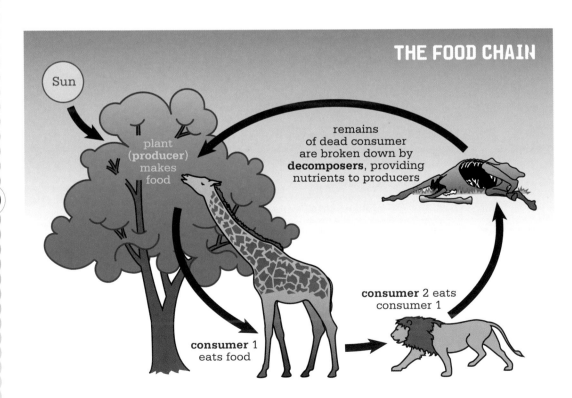

THE FOOD CHAIN

Sun

plant
(**producer**)
makes
food

remains
of dead consumer
are broken down by
decomposers, providing
nutrients to producers

consumer 2 eats
consumer 1

consumer 1
eats food

(roots, stems, etc.), but some is transferred to the consumers that eat them. In this way, the Sun's energy is passed on to the consumer. The process is not very efficient. Only about 10 percent of the energy is actually passed on to the next level. Grasshoppers, for example, store in their bodies only about 10 percent of the energy in the grass they eat. Sparrows store only about 10 percent of the energy they get from eating grasshoppers. Hawks store only about 10 percent of the energy they get by eating sparrows. (Imagine how much energy hawks would have if they could get all the energy in the original grass.)

When the animals and plants in this flow die, decomposers break down the remains. They release the energy remaining in the dead matter for their own use and produce heat that escapes to their surroundings. That is why energy is said to flow through the ecosystem. It is a one-way trip. However, being a flow is not a problem for the ecosystem because the Sun continually delivers fresh energy for the producers to capture and make into new food.

Other materials are cycled in a loop through the ecosystem. Water travels through the biosphere into the hydrosphere and then into the atmosphere and back again. The water cycle involves evaporation (into water vapor), condensation (into liquid water), precipitation, runoff, and evaporation again. While water is on the surface, it is used in a side loop by plants in photosynthesis and by other living things for building cells. Living things give off water, which eventually goes to other living things to be used again.

Carbon dioxide gas and oxygen gas cycle through the biosphere and atmosphere. Animals give off carbon dioxide as they breathe. The waste gas from animals—along with carbon dioxide given off by burning of forests and grasslands, oil, and natural gas—is taken in by plants and used in photosynthesis to make food and oxygen. Some of the oxygen is used by plants to release energy from their food for growth. The rest of the oxygen is given off as a waste gas that is used by animals for breathing and in combustion of fuels. Carbon

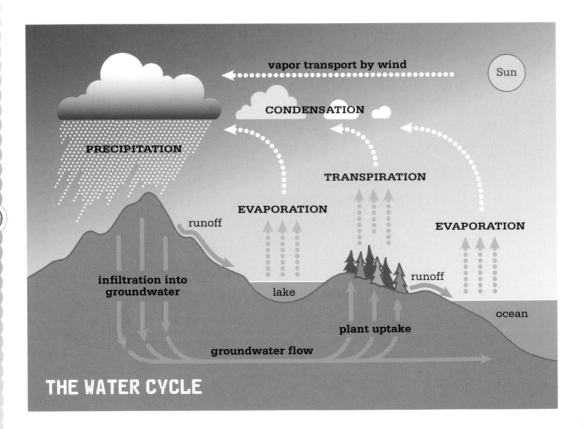

THE WATER CYCLE

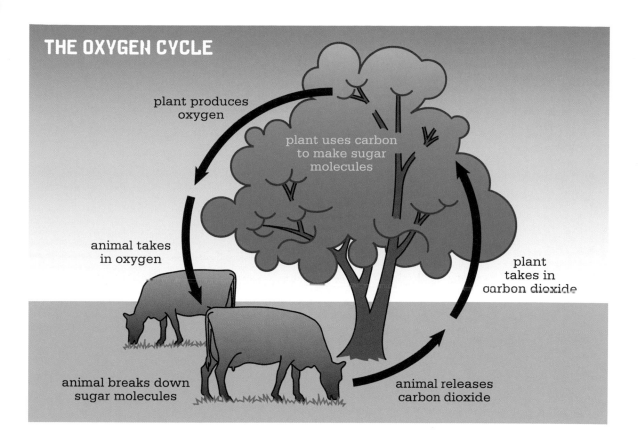

THE OXYGEN CYCLE

plant produces
oxygen

plant uses carbon
to make sugar
molecules

plant
takes in
carbon dioxide

animal takes
in oxygen

animal breaks down
sugar molecules

animal releases
carbon dioxide

dioxide and oxygen continually cycle through the
biosphere and atmosphere.

HELP OR HURT

A small version of cycles and flows occurs in a relationship
between organisms where two living things live in close
association. The association is called symbiosis. Some
forms of symbiosis are damaging, while others are benefi-
cial. A tree fungus needs a tree to grow on, but it dam-
ages the tree as it grows. A clown fish lives within the
poisonous tentacles of a sea anemone. The fish is immune
to the poison. The tentacles provide protection for the fish.

CANARY IN A CAGE

Coal miners in the nineteenth century led very difficult lives. They entered deep mines at dawn and didn't leave until after sunset. Coal dust infiltrated their lungs and every pore of their bodies. The work was backbreaking, and injuries were common.

One of the greatest hazards of the mines was the presence of explosive coal gas. The flames from miners' candles and mine lamps could ignite deadly explosions. The miners couldn't smell the gas until it was too late. Their solution was to take canaries in small cages into the mines. They would watch the canaries as they worked. Canaries are more susceptible to the gas than humans. If the canaries passed out, it meant that the gases were building up to dangerous levels. An explosion could happen at any moment, so it was time to get out.

Canaries are no longer used in mines, but remember that the living things that share the world with us can reflect the health of our environment. When animals and plants start disappearing from the places we live, something is happening that is detrimental to our entire community.

In this photo from 1965, a Welsh miner carries a canary in a cage out of a mine in South Wales. Canaries were used as a safety measure in mines. Because the birds are more sensitive to gases than humans, miners could watch the bird's reactions and know when gas was building up in the mine.

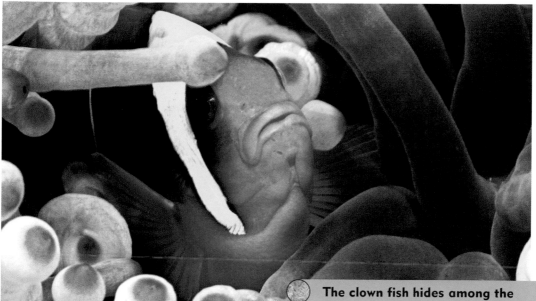

The clown fish hides among the poisonous tentacles of sea anemone. Clown fish live in the Red Sea, between the Arabian Peninsula and Africa. The sea has one of the most fascinating natural environments in the world.

The clown fish chases away predators that would eat the anemone. Both the clown fish and the anemone benefit. Humans have a symbiotic relationship with bacteria within our intestines. The bacteria help us digest our food while they get their energy from the food we eat. There are many symbiotic relationships in ecosystems.

BIOMES

Areas of Earth that have similar climates, similar physical properties, and similar communities of life are called biomes. Land biomes include forests, grasslands, and deserts. Water biomes include freshwater, marine, and estuarine biomes.

Far to the north of North America, Europe, and Asia is the tundra biome. This is a mostly treeless land of

Autumn color begins to take over the tundra in the Muldrow Glacier region of the Alaska Range.

mosses, grasses, and low shrubs.

Tundra animals include caribou, wolves, foxes, and hordes of blackflies and mosquitoes. Many birds feed there in summer but fly south in winter when the land is locked in ice and snow. South of the tundra is the taiga, which is a forested area of fir, pine, and spruce trees. The northern areas of the United States are taiga. Animals in this biome include deer, bears, moose, ducks, and geese.

Temperate deciduous forests spread in a wide swath across the United States, Europe, and Asia. Trees in this biome are primarily the broad-leaved kinds that drop their leaves in the fall. Chipmunks, squirrels, raccoons, deer, foxes, and bears live there, but it is also a biome heavily populated by humans. Over the past two hundred years, humans have cut down many of the trees to make room for farms and towns and hunted many of the animals to near extinction. New efforts to protect the land and regulate hunting have led to the recovery of some of the forests and a return of larger animals to some areas. But much of this biome is still unprotected.

The central portions of many continents are covered with grassland biomes. They have mostly low, grassy plants, with an occasional patch of trees. Grasslands are home to grazing animals such as American bison, gazelles, elephants, and wildebeests.

Among all the biomes, the tropical rain forests are probably the most important to humans. It is there, in the hot, rainy lands of the equatorial region of Earth, that more species of life are found than in all the other land biomes combined. Many of the animals that live there inhabit the massive trees. Flowers, vines, reptiles, amphibians, and monkeys are common.

Bison roam at Badlands National Park in South Dakota. This area of the United States is part of a grassland biome.

Biologists have discovered many chemicals manufactured by rain forest life that are used to treat disease. Rain forests are like exotic chemical factories. Unfortunately, rain forests are being cleared for roads and farms at an alarming rate. Without protection, the rain forests and thousands of species unique to them could all be gone by the end of this century.

Deserts are the last land biome, and they are the opposite of the rain forests. Deserts get only about one-tenth or one-hundredth the amount of rain that falls on a rain forest. The land is parched, but it is not devoid of life. Plants such as cacti have adapted to deserts by storing infrequent rainwater in thick, accordion-like stems and protecting themselves with thorns. Snakes, spiders, and scorpions are common in deserts.

The Sahara in northern Africa is the largest hot desert on Earth.

The freshwater biome consists of freshwater lakes and rivers. Many species of living things, such as bass, trout, frogs, salamanders, and a wide range of insects, live in the water. Such plants as duckweed float on the surface, while other plants grow from the bottom.

The world's largest living animals are blue whales, which can be 82 feet (25 m) long and weigh 132 tons (120 metric tons).

The marine biome differs from the freshwater biome in that it contains salty water. The marine biome includes all of the world's oceans and is home to many kinds of fish, mammals, shellfish, and crustaceans such as lobsters. The blue whale is the world's largest living animal. It eats tiny, shrimplike krill. It can be more than 100 feet (30 m) long and weigh more than 200 tons (180 metric tons). Many parts of the oceans are covered with floating phytoplankton. Phytoplankton is a major producer, through photosynthesis, of the world's oxygen supply.

Estuaries are a halfway house between the freshwater and marine biomes. Freshwater runoff enters the oceans and mixes with salt water to make a less salty home for grasses, crabs, shrimp, and birds. Many fishes use estuaries for hatching their eggs but live in the open ocean for the rest of their lives.

How are biomes and ecosystems related? Biomes are made up of ecosystems. Take the taiga biome. It hosts pine and spruce forests, lakes, rivers, pastures, mountains, and ice fields. Each of these features of a taiga is an ecosystem. They all interact with one another. How they interact can be demonstrated by tracing the flow of energy and chemicals. Start with an aspen tree. The tree captures the Sun's energy and makes food. An elk eats the leaves and bark of the tree. Eventually, a bear eats the elk. When the bear dies, smaller scavenger animals eat its body and decomposers break down the remains. Rains carry what is left into rivers and lakes where they add nutrients, enabling plants to grow. Birds eat the insects, fish, and amphibians that live off the freshwater plants. Then the birds migrate south in the winter. When they die, their remains are washed into estuaries and then into oceans. Plants and fish use the nutrients to grow. People harvest the fish for food.

As you can see, the relationships between ecosystems are very complex. Many cycles occur within cycles. So if human activities change an ecosystem, the effect is far reaching. Fill in a swamp to build a factory or a farm. Exterminate wolves because they occasionally prey on sheep. Destroy a grassland by having too many animals graze there. Clear-cut a forest for farms and roads. Dump chemicals in rivers and release noxious gases into the atmosphere. Use huge nets to catch entire populations of fish. Hunt the whales. All of these activities damage ecosystems, and the communities of life they host suffer. Remember that humans are a part of the ecosystems. What we do to them, we do to ourselves.

CONCLUSION

LIFE IN THE UNIVERSE

With its estimated thirty million species and perhaps hundreds of millions of extinct species, Earth is truly a fantastic planet. Many remarkable events had to occur for life to appear and thrive on Earth. Earth is the right size to have a gravitational field that is not too strong and not too weak, and it has liquid water, a thick atmosphere, and an abundance of organic chemicals. It is also a safe world where life has been able to evolve with relatively few disturbances.

Earth is part of a solar system of large and small planets. Earth is number three outward from the Sun. Earth is at the perfect distance from the Sun for life to thrive. But scientists now think that Earth could have been a much harsher environment if it weren't for planet five—Jupiter.

Jupiter's diameter is eleven times that of Earth, and Jupiter sweeps around the Sun in an orbit that takes nearly twelve years. *Sweep* is an appropriate word because of Jupiter's powerful gravity. As it travels around the Sun, Jupiter's gravity attracts comets and asteroids. It bends their orbits so that they are flung to more distant parts of the solar system. Because of Jupiter,

This computer artwork shows the relative size of Earth *(lower left)* compared to Jupiter, the largest planet in the solar system.

the inner solar system is relatively free of comets and asteroids that could collide with Earth. A chance collision with Earth could be devastating to all the life that the planet sustains.

As we look at all the conditions and events that shaped Earth, it would seem that Earth is a very rare occurrence, perhaps the only place where life is found. Still, scientists think that life might be relatively common throughout the universe. The reason is sheer numbers. Take the Milky Way galaxy, of which our Sun and its planets are a part. The Milky Way contains hundreds of billions of stars. If only 5 percent of all the stars in our galaxy have Earth-like planets, the Milky Way could be home to ten billion planetary systems with rocky planets like Earth. If some of those planets were at the right distance from their stars and had the right chemistry and a protective planet like Jupiter as a neighbor, the chances of life would be very good. The problem is finding those planets.

It would be great to hop onto *Star Trek's Enterprise* or *Star Wars' Millennium Falcon* and warp or hyperdrive our way on a sightseeing tour of the Milky Way. But we can't. We can barely send unmanned spacecraft to the planets in our own solar system. But scientists do have advanced optical and radio telescopes. Planets orbiting nearby stars in the galaxy are being discovered nearly every week. But that doesn't mean these planets have life on them. For the time being, the only way to communicate with other life is by radio.

Radio was discovered in the late 1800s. Since then, radio waves have been leaking away from Earth and heading out into the galaxy at the speed of light. If another world evolved intelligent life and that life discovered radio, radio waves would be streaming away from their planet too. Small teams of Earth's scientists have been using radio telescopes (big-dish antennae) to scan the stars for radio waves produced by intelligent life. In the forty years since scientists started searching, they have not detected any radio waves that weren't natural or accidentally produced by Earth's radio transmitters. This is not surprising, because even if scientists could rule out ten stars a day, 99.99999 percent of the stars in the Milky Way would still be left to investigate! Scientists have a big job ahead of them.

Scientists are more likely to discover life on Mars or on Jupiter's icy moon Europa. Mars once had a thicker atmosphere and liquid water running on its surface.

Radio telescopes, such as this one in Great Britain, allow scientists to listen for radio waves that could be produced by intelligent life on other planets.

It is likely to have bacteria-like life thriving beneath its surface, where water is still present. Europa is thought to have an ocean of liquid water beneath the cracked ice that covers the planet. The environment there could be like the life-rich, deepwater smoker vents beneath Earth's oceans.

If scientists do find life or signs of ancient life on Mars or Europa or even somewhere else, they will learn more about life on Earth as well. Scientists may learn how life appeared on those worlds. Mars, for example, doesn't have a thick atmosphere and running water on its surface as it did in the past. If there is still life on Mars, scientists will learn how it adapted to worldwide environmental changes. That information could be very important to help us cope with changes that will surely take place on Earth. On other worlds, scientists may find clues that will enable us to solve the greatest mystery of our biosphere—how the molecules in the organic soup of early Earth found the spark of life.

GLOSSARY

amino acids: molecules that are the building blocks for proteins

Animalia: the kingdom of animals

Archaea: the kingdom of single-celled organisms without nuclei that live in harsh environments

atoms: the smallest particle of an element that can exist and still have all the properties of that element

biomes: areas of Earth that have similar climates, similar physical properties, and similar communities of life

cell: the fundamental unit of life

cell membrane: the barrier that surrounds a cell

cellulose: the primary porous material that makes up the wall of a plant cell

chlorophyll: a green pigment that captures the energy in sunlight for the process of photosynthesis

cilia: small hairlike projections extending outward from unicellular organisms that bend and wave to help the organism move

community: all the species of life within an ecosystem

consumers: living members of an ecosystem that obtain the energy to live by feeding on other living things

cycle: closed or circular path of nutrients or gases through an ecosystem

decomposers: living members of an ecosystem that break down dead matter

DNA (deoxyribonucleic acid): the material inside the nucleus of a cell that carries genetic information

ecology: the science of the interaction of living things with one another and with their environment

ecosystem: a smaller unit within a biome consisting of all the living and nonliving components in a given area, such as a desert or a pond

enzymes: chemicals that speed up chemical reactions

Eubacteria: the kingdom of single-celled organisms without nuclei that thrive in moderate environments

extinct: the complete dying off of an entire species of life

flow: one-way movement of resources through an ecosystem

fossil: the remains, or traces, of ancient life, usually turned to stone

Fungi: the kingdom of plantlike organisms that lack chlorophyll and obtain nutrients from living or decaying organic matter

gene: a segment of DNA that provides instructions for protein formation; the basic biological unit of heredity

genetic: a characteristic that can be passed from one generation to another through genes

homeostasis: the process in which living things maintain internal conditions in spite of changes in the environment

hypothesis: a proposed statement, which scientists test, that explains some event in nature

mass extinction: a period in the history of Earth in which thousands or millions of species of life became extinct within a relatively short period of time

nucleus: the central control center of animal and plant cells

organelles: structures within cells that perform specialized functions

paleontologist: a scientist who studies the fossil remains of ancient life to learn how the organisms lived and what their environment was like

photosynthesis: the process of using energy from the Sun to convert water and carbon dioxide into food and oxygen

phytoplankton: floating microscopic plants and animals. Some experts expand this definition to include all floating plants, such as kelp.

Plantae: the kingdom of plants

producer: an organism that makes its own food from inorganic substances

protein: a complex molecule made up of one or more chains of amino acids. Proteins perform a wide variety of functions in cells.

Protista: the kingdom of single-celled organisms that have nuclei

RNA (ribonucleic acid): a chemical similar to DNA that translates DNA's genetic code into proteins

species: a group of living things that share common characteristics and are able to breed with one another and produce offspring that can also breed

spores: the reproductive cells of fungi, nonflowering plants such as ferns and mosses, and some single-celled organisms

symbiosis: a close relationship between two organisms where one or both benefit from the relationship

BIBLIOGRAPHY

Haines, Tim, and Paul Chambers. *The Complete Guide to Prehistoric Life*. Buffalo: Firefly Books, 2006.

Layman, Dale. *Biology Demystified—a Self-Teaching Guide*. New York: McGraw-Hill, 2003.

Miller, Kenneth R., and Joseph S. Levine. *Biology*. Upper Saddle River, NJ: Prentice Hall, 2000.

Smithsonian Institution. *Animal—The Definitive Visual Guide to the World's Wildlife*. London: Dorling Kindersley, 2005.

Thain, Michael, and Michael Hickman. *Dictionary of Biology*. 11th ed. London: Penguin Reference, 2004.

FOR FURTHER INFORMATION

Books

Ackroyd, Peter. *Voyages Through Time: The Beginning*. New York: DK Children, 2004.

Banquieri, Eduardo. *The Biosphere*. New York: Chelsea House Publications, 2005.

Burnie, David. *Endangered Planet*. Boston: Kingfisher, 2004.

Fleisher, Paul. *The Big Bang*. Minneapolis: Twenty-First Century Books, 2006.

Koppes, Steven. *Killer Rocks from Outer Space*. Minneapolis: Twenty-First Century Books, 2004.

Miller, Ron. *Earth and the Moon*. Minneapolis: Twenty-First Century Books, 2003.

Nardo, Don. *The Search for Extraterrestrial Life*. Farmington Hills, MI: Lucent Books, 2006.

Silverstein, Alvin, Virginia Silverstein, and Laura Silverstein Nunn. *Cells*. Minneapolis: Twenty-First Century Books, 2002.

Walker, Richard. *Microscopic Life*. Boston: Kingfisher, 2004.

Winner, Cherie. *Life on the Edge*. Minneapolis: Lerner Publications Company, 2006.

Websites

Astrobiology Web.com. "Life in Extreme Environments."
http://www.astrobiology.com/extreme.html
Astrobiology Web provides curious students and teachers with information about life-forms that live in extreme environments.

Public Broadcasting System, NOVA website. "Origins: Journey Back to the Beginning of Everything: The Universe, Earth, and Life Itself."
http://www.pbs.org/wgbh/nova/origins
Nova is a website with links that provide information on a variety of scientific topics.

University of California Museum of Paleontology. "What Killed the Dinosaurs? The Great Mystery." http://www.ucmp.berkeley.edu/diapsids/extinction.html
The mystery of the dinosaurs unfolds on this website, which charts the historical events that led to dinosaur's extinction.

University of California Museum of Paleontology. "The World's Biomes." http://www.ucmp.berkeley.edu/glossary/gloss5/biome/index.html
Visitors to this site will find a discussion of the five biomes on Earth. Links take viewers to pages with information on aquatics, deserts, forests, grasslands and the tundra.

INDEX

ABOUT THE AUTHOR

Gregory L. Vogt holds a doctor of education degree in curriculum and instruction from Oklahoma State University. He began his professional career as a science teacher. He later joined NASA's education programs. He works in outreach programs for the Kennedy Space Center. He also serves as an educational consultant to Delaware North Parks Services of Spaceport. Vogt has written more than seventy children's science books.

PHOTO ACKNOWLEDGMENTS

The images in this book are used with the permission of: PhotoDisc Royalty Free by Getty Images, (lava: center ring), (cracked earth: second ring), (vegetation: main and fourth ring), (sky/clouds: fifth ring), all backgrounds, pp. 2–3, 6, 8, 19, 30, 31, 32, 33, 36, 44, 52, 54, 56, 67, 69; MedioImages Royalty Free by Getty Images, (water: third ring), all backgrounds, p. 2; NASA (stars/nebula: sixth ring), (earth), all backgrounds, pp. 2–3; © Laura Westlund/Independent Picture Service, pp. 8, 25, 58, 60, 61; National Park Service, pp. 10, 65; © Eric V. Grave/ Photo Researchers, Inc., p. 12; © LSHTM/Photo Researchers, Inc., p. 13; © Henry Guttmann/Hulton Archive/Getty Images, p. 16; © Dr. Ken MacDonald/ Photo Researchers, Inc., p. 17; © George Musil/Visuals Unlimited, p. 22; © Michael Abbey/Photo Researchers, Inc., p. 24; © Jeff Rotman/Photo Researchers, Inc., p. 26; © Steve Austin; Papilio/CORBIS, p. 28; © Robert W. Domm/Visuals Unlimited, p. 29; © Detlev van Ravenswaay/Photo Researchers, Inc., pp. 34, 53; © John Reader/Photo Researchers, Inc., p. 37; © Bettmann/CORBIS, p. 38; © Digital Art/CORBIS, p. 40; © Science VU/Visuals Unlimited, p. 42; © Annie Griffiths Belt/CORBIS, p. 45; © A. J. Copley/Visuals Unlimited, p. 47; © Claus Lunau/Bonnier Pub./Photo Researchers, Inc., p. 51; © Martin Wendler/ Photo Researchers, Inc., p. 55; © Laister/Express/Hulton Archive/Getty Images, p. 62; © Tarik Tinazay/AFP/Getty Images, p. 63; © Charles Mauzy/CORBIS, p. 64; © Jane Thomas/Visuals Unlimited, p. 66; © Victor Habbick Visions/Photo Researchers, Inc., p. 70; © Jodrell Bank Observatory/AFP/Getty Images, p. 72. Front Cover: PhotoDisc Royalty Free by Getty Images, (lava: center ring), (cracked earth: second ring), (vegetation: main and fourth ring), (sky/clouds: fifth ring); MedioImages Royalty Free by Getty Images, (water: third ring); NASA, (stars/nebula: sixth ring). Back Cover: PhotoDisc Royalty Free by Getty Images, (vegetation); NASA, (earth). Spine: PhotoDisc Royalty Free by Getty Images, (vegetation).